DINOSAURS
Sticker Book

Marks and Spencer p.l.c.
PO Box 3339
Chester CH99 9QS

shop online
www.marksandspencer.com

ISBN 978-1-78445-301-5
Printed in China

M&S
KIDS

The Dinosaur Museum

The word 'dinosaur' is Greek for 'terrible lizard'! At least 700 types of dinosaur have been discovered and named, but what actually were dinosaurs?

Mesozoic

Dinosaurs lived in the Mesozoic –245 to 65 million years ago. No single species lived this long; most only survived 1 to 2 million years. The Mesozoic splits into three periods; the Triassic, Jurassic and Cretaceous. The maps below show how continents changed during this time.

Triassic – 245 to 208 million years ago

Jurassic – 208 to 144 million years ago

Cretaceous – 144 to 65 million years ago

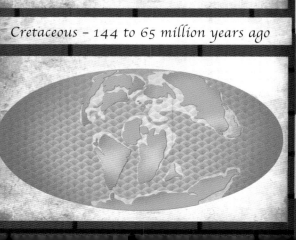

The Triassic – 245 to 208 million years ago

When the earliest dinosaurs appeared in the Late Triassic Period, all land was joined in one giant 'supercontinent'. Away from the more humid coast the land was hot, dry and dusty, and volcanoes were common.

Plants included horsetails, mosses, seed ferns and cycads ... but no flowers or grass!

Herrerasaurus (her-rare-rah-saw-rus)
From South America, this 3-metre long dinosaur preyed on small plant eaters. Teeth marks in a fossil show it could have been lunch for a massive reptile like Saurosuchus.

Staurikosaurus (staw-rick-oh-saw-rus)
From South America, Staurikosaurus was about 2 metres long, and weighed about 30 kilograms. It hunted in packs, targeting prey larger than itself.

Eudimorphodon (you-dye-mor-foh-don)
Eudimorphodon had a 1-metre wide wingspan, and sharp teeth ideal for catching fish, or flying insects.

Saurosuchus
(saw-roh-sue-kus)

The first mammals had evolved. They were small, mostly nocturnal, ate insects and tried to stay out of the way of dinosaurs!

Mussaurus (moo-saw-rus)
From South America, this 3-metre long dinosaur belonged to the sauropod family, like the famous Brachiosaurus.

Z
z z
z

Create your own Triassic sticker scene!

Z
z
z

Coelophysis (seel–oh–fie–sis)

From North America, the 3-metre long Coelophysis belonged to the theropod family, like the famous Tyrannosaurus rex. Its name means 'hollow form', due to its hollow bones that kept it lightweight and fast. We now know all theropods had hollow bones.

Coelophysis hunted in packs.

Stick a Coelophysis here to complete the pack!

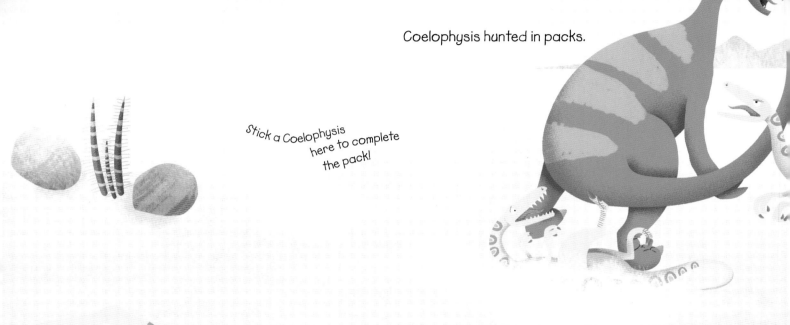

Sharp, backward-pointing teeth for tearing at prey.

A narrow head and large front-facing eyes gave excellent vision ... I hope they don't spot me!

Plateosaurus (plat-ee-oh-saw-rus)

The Plateosaurus is one of the best-known Triassic dinosaurs. Found in Europe, these vegetarians lived in herds, and measured between 5 and 10 metres long. At night they stayed close together to keep safe from predators.

Long neck meant this was one of the first dinosaurs that could eat treetop vegetation.

Eyes on the side of the head gave a wide field of vision.

Long tail for balance.

These Plateosaurus are stuck! Place a sinking dinosaur here!

The fossils of a herd of Plateosaurus have been found, all standing upright. They probably got stuck in mud and died.

The Jurassic – 208 to 144 million years ago

As the supercontinent split, coastlines grew longer and hot, dusty interiors became cooler and more humid. Lush forests of rain-soaked conifers and ginkgoes covered much of the planet, providing food for gigantic sauropods like Brachiosaurus.

Pterodactylus (terr-ah-dak-til-us)
Found in Europe and Africa – probably the best of all Jurassic fliers.

Dinosaur teeth were replaceable. When one fell out, another one grew to take its place.

Ceratosaurus (sair-rah-toh-saw-rus)
From North America, this 6-metre long carnivore had impressive horns above its nose and eyes.

Archaeopteryx
(arr-kay-opp-ter-rix)
Found in Europe, this is thought to be the earliest known bird. It had a long, bony tail and teeth like a reptile.

Create your own Jurassic sticker scene!

A very big lunch!

Found in North America, Apatosaurus (ah-pat-oh-saw-rus) was a true giant. At 23 metres long, and weighing around 25 tonnes, its size and herd behaviour was protection against most predators. A predator's best chance of a meal was to separate one of the smaller members of the herd.

Apatosaurus' long tail was made up of 82 bones and could swing quickly from side to side.

Allosaurus (al-oh-saw-rus)
Found in North America, Africa and Europe, this 12-metre long carnivore was a typical example of the carnivorous theropod family.

Stegosaurus (stegg-oh-saw-rus)

The 9-metre long Stegosaurus was found in North America. Scientists used to think the plates on its back were protective armour. Newer theories suggest they may have flushed red with blood to attract a mate or scare off predators!

90-centimetre long tailspikes were a dangerous weapon!

Add Stegosaurus' protective plates and tail spikes!

Stegosaurus' brain was only the size of a walnut ... but with a maximum speed of 7 kilometres per hour it didn't have to think too fast!

Stegosaurus chomped through low-growing plants with its tough beak.

Compsognathus (komp-sog-nay-thus)

Carnivorous dinosaurs are usually shown as ferocious giants crashing through prehistoric forests. But smaller hunters, like the chicken-sized Compsognathus (found in Europe) were just as deadly in their own way! These little dinosaurs were quick, agile, and had a mouth full of sharp teeth.

Fill the scene with tasty dragonflies!

Long tail used for balance and stability when chasing prey.

Sharp teeth perfect for catching small prey like lizards and flying insects.

Claws on short forelimbs could be used to hold prey.

Compsognathus fossils are found in coastal habitats. They may have lived on islands, separated from other dinosaur species.

The Cretaceous – 144 to 65 million years ago

The Cretaceous saw dinosaurs at their most diverse. As the continents separated, new species evolved on each land mass. The giant sauropods like Brachiosaurus were replaced by smaller plant eaters. Huge pterosaurs flew in the skies, massive reptiles lived in the water, but dinosaurs still ruled the land!

Chasmosaurus (kaz-muh-saw-rus)
From North America – its large bony head frill was for defence and display.

Parasaurolophus (pah-rah-saw-roh-loh-fuss)
From North America, the hollow crest of this 10-metre long hadrosaur may have been used for bellowing!

The first flowering plants appeared including early roses, magnolias and water lilies.

The lush forests were the perfect habitat for insects and small reptiles ... *yummy!*

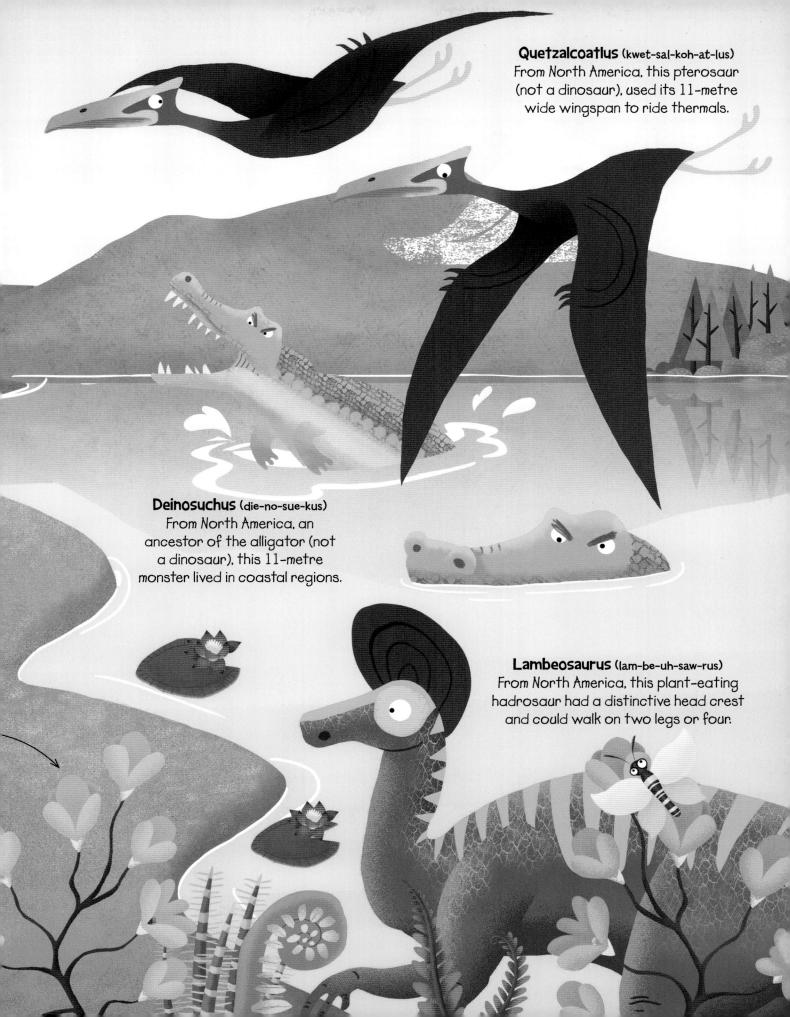

Quetzalcoatlus (kwet-sal-koh-at-lus)
From North America, this pterosaur (not a dinosaur), used its 11-metre wide wingspan to ride thermals.

Deinosuchus (die-no-sue-kus)
From North America, an ancestor of the alligator (not a dinosaur), this 11-metre monster lived in coastal regions.

Lambeosaurus (lam-be-uh-saw-rus)
From North America, this plant-eating hadrosaur had a distinctive head crest and could walk on two legs or four.

Create your own Cretaceous sticker scene!

Iguanodon (igg-wan-oh-don)

This 10-metre long herbivore was found in many parts of the world. Its incredible hands were uniquely designed. The three central fingers ended in hooves for walking, the flexible fifth finger was used to grasp plants, but most impressive of all was its huge thumb spike - a defensive weapon against predators!

A tough beak chomped through tough plants which were chewed before swallowing.

Stick a hungry T. rex here.

Large adults usually walked on four legs and juveniles on two.

Fossilized tracks suggest Iguanodons travelled in herds.

Iguanodons were a successful species of dinosaur found in both Europe and North America.

Maiasaura (my-ah-saw-rah)

This plant-eating hadrosaur was found in North America. 'Maiasaura' means 'good mother lizard'- they were caring mothers, looking after their eggs and hatchlings carefully. 9-metre long Maiasaura lived in herds numbering up to 10,000 and nested in colonies – a bit like seabirds today.

Hatchlings stayed in the nest after they were born and were fed by their mum.

Just 40 centimetres at birth, they grew very rapidly.

Stick a Maiasaura hatchling here!

No dinosaur egg larger than a basketball has ever been found!

Stick a Maiasaura egg here!

Stick a Maiasaura egg here!

Maiasaura filled their nests with bits of plants. As the plants rotted, they kept the eggs warm.

Battle to the death!

Triceratops' (tri-ser-uh-tops) size, neck armour and horns protected it from most predators. But to a hungry Tyrannosaurus rex (tye-ran-uh-saw-rus rex) a young Triceratops looked like a tasty meal! But this was a battle to the death – Triceratops' horns could easily inflict a fatal wound.

Triceratops
From North America, this huge vegetarian was 9 metres long and very heavy!

Head frill up to 1.8 metres wide.

Sharp, 1-metre long, front-facing horns.

Stick a baby Triceratops here.

Stick a baby Triceratops here.

Stick a baby Triceratops here.

Pachycephalosaurus (pack-ee-sef-uh-loh-saw-rus)

From North America, this 8-metre long dinosaur was a real head-banger! Its name means 'thick-headed reptile', because the top of an adult's skull could grow to an amazing 25 centimetres thick! It's thought these super-strong skulls were used for fighting to determine social status and mating rights.

Bony heads could also be used to charge and batter predators.

Stick a Pachycephalosaurus here.

Scientists now think Pachycephalosaurus tried to bash an opponent's sides rather than its head.

Small knobs and spikes covered much of the head for extra protection.

Not many fossils have been found, possibly because Pachycephalosaurus lived in rocky areas where fossils formed less easily.

Ankylosaurus (an-kile-oh-saw-rus)

At 9 metres long and weighing around 6 tonnes, an Ankylosaurus was the armoured tank of the dinosaur world. Found in North America, Ankylosaurus' incredible armour and clubbed tail made them almost impossible to attack!

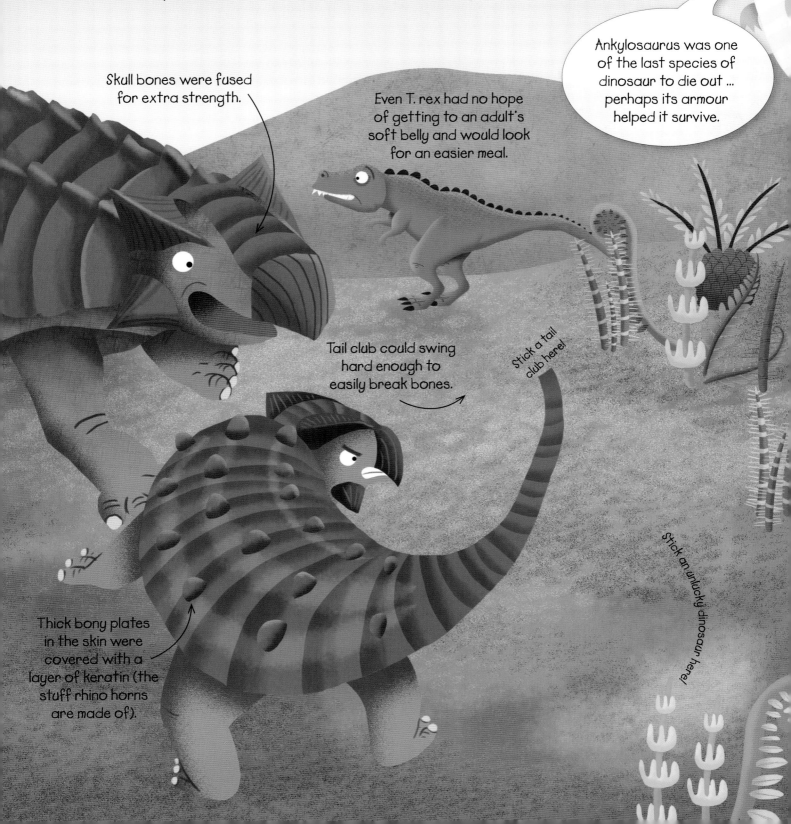

Skull bones were fused for extra strength.

Even T. rex had no hope of getting to an adult's soft belly and would look for an easier meal.

Ankylosaurus was one of the last species of dinosaur to die out ... perhaps its armour helped it survive.

Tail club could swing hard enough to easily break bones.

Stick a tail club here!

Stick an unlucky dinosaur here!

Thick bony plates in the skin were covered with a layer of keratin (the stuff rhino horns are made of).

The doom of the dinosaurs!

No one knows for certain why, but 65 million years ago, dinosaurs became extinct. The most likely reason was the impact of a giant asteroid. This may not have been the only cause, and other theories suggest massive volcanoes or a more gradual process caused by changes in climate or environment.

A blanket of dust, smoke and cloud would have kept the planet in freezing darkness for months.

75 per cent of species became extinct, including pterosaurs and most marine reptiles.

Without sunlight, plants would have died, causing the starvation of herbivores and then carnivores.

Dinosaur hunting

Nobody has ever seen a living dinosaur. It's the job of a palaeontologist (pay-lee-ohn-tol-oh-gyst) to excavate and preserve fossils and to try to learn about the dinosaur they came from. Finding a whole skeleton is rare. Many species are only known from a single tooth or bone!

Dinosaur sizes are estimates based on fossils. Facts can change with new discoveries!

Footprints tell us a lot about dinosaurs' lives. These large prints are from a sauropod. The smaller prints are from a theropod, hunting its prey.

When a bone is discovered, the surrounding earth and rock is carefully scraped away to reveal any other bones.

The best places to find fossils are in deserts made up of sedimentary rock.

Many dinosaurs were named wrongly. What was called 'Brontosaurus' is now agreed to be Apatosaurus.

Use the stickers to fill in the missing bones!

Most dinosaurs are found by amateurs, not palaeontologists! Maybe one day you'll discover your own species!

The Dinosaur
Museum

Triassic sticker scene

Jurassic sticker scene